Mrs. Ballard's Parrots

OTHER BOOKS BY ARNE SVENSON

Prisoners

Sock Monkeys (200 out of 1,863) (with Ron Warren)

Mrs. Ballard's Parrots

ARNE SVENSON

HARRY N. ABRAMS, INC., PUBLISHERS

For Charles and for Evelyn

EDITOR: Deborah Aaronson
DESIGNER: Laura Lindgren
PRODUCTION MANAGER: Jane Searle

Library of Congress Cataloging-in-Publication Data
Svenson, Arne.
  Mrs. Ballard's parrots / Arne Svenson.
    p.   cm.
  ISBN 0-8109-5886-4
    1. Photography of birds. 2. Parrots–Showing–Pictorial works. 3. Ballard, Alba, 1928–1994. 4. Decoration and ornament. 5. Stage props–Pictorial works. 6. Costume designers–United States–Biography. I. Title.
  TR729.B5.S85 2005
  779'.092–dc22   2004023436

Printed and bound in China
10 9 8 7 6 5 4 3 2 1

Harry N. Abrams, Inc.
100 Fifth Avenue
New York, N.Y. 10011
www.abramsbooks.com

Abrams is a subsidiary of

LA MARTINIÈRE
G R O U P E

Contents

Introduction

In the summer of 1992, my friends Hap and Liza were spending a few weeks in Gstaad, Switzerland, staying in Liza's childhood home. While there, they came across an envelope containing a series of snapshots that had been sent by a fan in the early 1970s to Liza's mother and stepfather—Elizabeth Taylor and Richard Burton. Included was a brief letter by the admirer, but this was lost soon after the photographs were discovered, and no one who saw it can remember the specific contents of the note or the name of the sender.

Hap and Liza brought the photographs back to New York. Knowing my voracious appetite for acquiring unique and odd images taken by amateur and anonymous photographers, my friends told me they had some snapshots to add to my collection. But they didn't forewarn me about the subject matter—how could they? It would have ruined the surprise that awaited me when I first opened the box.

At the top of the stack of snapshots was a picture of two parrots dressed in leather jackets, fringed pants, and wigs, perched atop little motorcycles, one bird flashing the peace sign, the other smoking a cigarette, with tiny humanlike fabric hands that appeared to be sewn onto the cuffs of the leather jackets. The background for this scene was a painted set of a bank, and written in ballpoint pen on the top margin of the photograph was "Easy Rider..!" (plate 5). The next picture was captioned "Here Come the Bride..!" (plate 22). In this image a small yellow parrot was dressed as a bride with a flowing veil, a bouquet, and a blond wig, while a second bird, the groom, green with red eyes, sported a fine tuxedo. The couple stood before a painted church backdrop, and three angelic human dolls floated rather ominously over the birds' heads. Each subsequent photo in this stack of fifty or so was the same: parrots in elaborate costumes reenacting scenes from famous movies, television, history, storybooks, and 1970s popular culture.

I had never seen anything like these photographs. They possessed the raw quality of a grammar school theatrical production, except that birds, rather than children, inexplicably had been cast in the leading roles. I felt I had stumbled down Alice's rabbit hole and was privy to another dimension, a world in which a parrot dressed like Cher could nonchalantly chat with parrot Sonny in the local pizza joint (plate 4), and nobody would bat an eye.

❄

Curiously, among the images of parrots there were also five photos of a very attractive woman taken at different times in different locales. In one she stands lakeside holding a small bird alongside a parrot on a perch, and in another she holds a dog and a bird and is kneeling next to a young boy with a cat. I could only assume that this woman must be the creator of the parrot photographs. The letter originally accompanying the photos having been lost, these five pictures and the date 1971 printed on the back of each photo became my only clues as to the origin of this work.

Nearly twelve years after I received the pictures, on a whim, I decided to try to find the woman I assumed had created them. Having no idea where in the world this woman might be, I started my quest by using the Internet. My first attempt, "BIRD COSTUMES," yielded more than 2,500 entries with such descriptive snippets as "Bird Seed Sale—Need loaders and people to dress in BIRD COSTUMES . . ." and "He was a very dignified personage in spite of his BIRD COSTUME." After an unfruitful review of hundreds more entries in this category, I refined my search to "PARROT COS-

TUMES," which provided me with arcane information such as "THEN I read in one of my parrot books recently that 'people dressed in PARROT COSTUMES are terrifying to parrots.' So. . . ."

After many more futile attempts, amusing though they were, I typed in "COSTUMES FOR PARROTS" and was rewarded with just one entry: *Slightly Jewish Movies* ". . . who still do Borscht-belt schtick, a couple who make animal sculptures out of balloons, and even a lady who makes outrageous COSTUMES FOR PARROTS are just some...." Encouraged, I went to the site and discovered this was a description of the acts represented by a talent agent character in Woody Allen's 1984 movie *Broadway Danny Rose.* I rented the movie, set the picture of the woman and her parrots next to the television, and watched for her to show up in the film. In the final scene, all Danny's acts attend a party in his apartment. And there, seated on a couch beside a costumed bird on a perch, was the woman in the photos. I couldn't believe I had found her, and I was even more delighted when the credits rolled by: "Bird Lady": played by Alba Ballard. Finally I had a name.

Resuming my Internet search, I now typed in "Alba Ballard." A number of sites turned up referencing her appearance in *Broadway Danny Rose;* however, one site stood out. It was an article about veterinarian Dr. Jonathan Greenfield, who had been the host of a Long Island, New York, cable show called *The Family Pet Show.* When asked who had been his favorite guest on the show, he replied, "I really never had [one]. They are all so interesting. I do remember one in particular: Alba Ballard. She was such a charming lady, who dressed her parrots in the most beautiful costumes. She had a very strong Italian accent and always laughed. Ballard was so proud of her work, and proud she should have been. The costumes were exquisite and so were her birds. Unfortunately, she passed away some years ago, but she will be missed."

Dr. Greenfield's statement told me more than I thought I could ever have known about the woman with the parrots. I contacted Dr. Greenfield, and he gave me a list of people who had known or sometimes worked with Alba throughout the years. Through these contacts I was able to locate Alba's husband, Marvin, and their son, Claudio, both of whom were able to answer many of the questions I had about her life and art. I also gained valuable insights from pet expert Marc Marrone, who grew up near the Ballards and credits Alba with teaching him most of what he knows about parrots.

❄

Alba Ballard was born Alba Spinetto on May 6, 1928, in Porto Tolle, Rovigio, Italy, the sixth child of Remondo and Olga Spinetto. The Spinettos were a theatrical family, and early in life Alba joined her parents and siblings in their variety stage troupe, Compagnia Spinetto. Singing, dancing, and comedy shows were on the bill as well as various animal acts. Even as a girl, Alba exhibited a special talent in gaining the trust of the animals with which she worked. This trust even extended to undomesticated animals: at some point in her childhood, Alba's father and brother found a stray baby wolf, which Alba tamed and turned into a pet she named Bobi. She even made a little sleigh so that she could ride in the winter snow pulled by Bobi.

Alba's father died during World War II, and she took it upon herself to care for her family, often riding her bicycle into the countryside, foraging for food and fuel, hiding under bridges in freezing water when enemy aircraft would fly overhead. She had many run-ins with the German army; Alba recounted one instance when she was discovered hiding under a bridge by German soldiers and forced to assist in a crude appendectomy that was being performed on a soldier. The only instruments available to Alba and the soldiers were shards of glass from a shattered wine bottle broken when used to hit the soldier over the head to anesthetize him.

Post wartime life was also extremely arduous for the Spinetto family, but Alba eventually found a job working in the American PX in the small town of Vicenza. In 1956 Alba met her future husband, Marvin Ballard, in a Vicenza dance club. Marvin, an American working with the army as a contract engineer, and Alba were married in 1957 and their son, Claudio (pictured with Alba at right), was born in 1958.

In 1963 the Ballard family moved to the United States. After a stay in California, they relocated to Long Island, New York. As Marvin recalls,

It was at this time that Alba started her hobby of dressing birds in costume. She acquired a small yellow head caique and thought that it would be cute to make a costume for it.

Animals had always trusted her implicitly, and it did not take Alba long to convince her bird to lie down, stand still, and generally follow commands. Over time she acquired many other birds of various types such as cockatoos, macaws, etc. Eventually, Alba had more than fifty domestic and exotic birds in her care, though she only used ten to twenty for her costumed productions and photographs. In the old days she would use snaps to fasten the costume onto the birds, later switching to Velcro. The costumes slipped off and on easily, so if a bird became restless, Alba merely had to unfasten the back and slip the outfit off. The birds always loved the attention they received when starring in one of Alba's productions.

Alba developed a unique method of soaking felt in household glue and then molding it into various shapes to make costumes and humanlike legs, arms, and hands. Once the form was made, she would construct the costumes using materials and notions that she had collected in fabric stores, toy stores, and flea markets. Marvin was enlisted to make props and construct stage sets—often he would arrive home from work to be surprised by Alba with a list of what that evening's photo shoot should look like. He also was the principal photographer and, being an amateur, still feels he didn't do justice to her efforts.

Most of the images were shot in a spare bedroom Marvin had outfitted with a shooting platform made of plywood, spotlights that had been mounted on the ceiling, and a sliding, hinged latticework backdrop to which painted backgrounds could be affixed. Under Alba's direction, Marvin would construct elaborate props such as the piano and motorcycle (see, for example, plates 9 and 25), which Alba would embellish with decorations. Many nights the entire family would stay up until two or three in the morning perfecting the stage sets, cajoling the birds into position, and shooting the pictures. When Alba saw a movie she enjoyed, she would come home and start planning a parrot reenactment of pivotal scenes from the film (see, for example, plates 16–20, 42–43). She drew inspiration too from television shows and commercials of the day, such as a 1970s commercial for the woman's deodorant Soft and Dry (plate 8).

In addition to the photographs, Alba and Marvin also started making 16mm movie shorts. One such film was "The First Bird on the Moon," about which Marvin recalls, "Claudio built a bird-size lunar lander, and we rigged cable up in the garage and shot a reasonably good movie of the descent and the first claw print on the moon."

Alba's passion for her art was matched by a sense of obligation to entertain people. Alba's friends encouraged her to show off her talent, and she began bringing the costumed birds to schools, nursing homes, libraries, and even to office parties and bar mitzvahs. Alba was very expository; she loved putting on the whole show, and was dedicated to making the best show possible. Often this entailed numerous birds, costume changes, and sometimes Claudio working as her assistant. Her shows brought levity to those fortunate enough to see them, and Marvin recalls an incident at a mental hospital when a longtime resident who had not spoken for fifteen years suddenly began to utter intelligible words upon hearing the talking birds in Alba's act. That Alba had taught the birds to sing and curse probably aided in the dramatic reception the act would often receive.

Love of her parrots, and indeed animals of all kind, was a guiding force in Alba's life. Despite having dozens of her own domesticated and wild birds to care for, she would babysit neighbors' and friends' pets, and when summoned by a worried owner, performed simple medical procedures on their wounded or sick birds. She even acted as veterinary assistant in a surgery for cancer on one of her parrots; the operation was conducted on her kitchen table and was deemed a great success by the doctor.

Alba worked as her own theatrical agent, sending out brochures, photos, and letters to numerous casting agents and television stations. She received numerous rejections, but now and again a call would come in for a commercial or TV appearance. In the early 1980s she had heard that Woody Allen was holding auditions for a movie for which he was looking for unusual acts—hence her appearance in *Broadway Danny Rose.*

Hoping to get Alba and the parrots on television, Marvin sent a copy of their film "The First Bird on the Moon" to Saturday Night Live in the late 1970s. The producers were excited enough with what they saw to send a camera crew to the Ballards' house and shoot the birds performing Alba-directed costumed dramas. This material was edited and narrated by Bill Murray in a marvelous send-up skit about the network's following season's programming. In the mid-1980s Alba and her parrots appeared several times on *Late Night with David Letterman,* always to rousing applause. A fan writing on the Internet recalls, "My all-time favorite Letterman guest, on the NBC show, was Alba Ballard, an eccentric elderly woman who dressed parrots up in costumes.

She appeared on the show around Thanksgiving one year in the mid-1980s with two turkeys whom she had dressed up as Ronald Reagan and Tip O'Neill." Or, as *Newsweek* reported "... you are less likely to see (Daniel) Moynihan on tonight's *Late Night* than Alba Ballard, a lady who dresses her pet parrots in tiny hand-sewn costumes for no apparent reason."

Alba continued working with her birds, appearing at charity events, and tirelessly

thinking up ingenious ways to showcase her talents until she suffered a stroke and then passed away on July 21, 1994. Sadly, all of the costumes and films and all but a handful of the photographs were lost after Alba's death.

᙭

Alba Ballard was a unique artist who created a fantastical world unto itself. With no formal training, she was able to achieve what many artists cannot—a comprehensible visual language with which to communicate with the world at large. Although the parrot-centric work may at first strike many as bizarre, it seems, from everything I have learned about Alba, to have been a most appropriate medium for her to have developed. She managed to meld her love of birds, her childhood background in the theater, and her amusement with popular culture into singular images that not only make us laugh, but also stir a kind of wistfulness for things past. Alba infused her projects with the same qualities she embraced in life: exuberance, tenacity, sincerity, and a wicked sense of humor.

When I envision Alba and her family late into the night coaxing two absurdly dressed parrots to lie in a lacy pink bed surrounded by bedside tables replete with a tiny champagne bottle and miniature lamps, I am not quite sure if I should be laughing out loud or crying over the intense earnestness of it all. She  wanted so badly to be recognized, to be famous for her art, but I think that people's perception of the eccentricity inherent in the work ultimately blocked an appreciation of it on other levels.

Looking at Alba's photos I know I am looking at the work of an artist, who, like so many contemporary artists, created artificial, staged worlds to make perceptible to the rest of us the possible reality they envision. And what a marvelous, surreal world it is: a winged Tiny Tim and Miss Vicky are back together again; General Patton is green, wounded—and molting just a bit; and Liberace, his white feathers a perfect complement to his gold brocade jacket and exquisitely bejeweled felt hands, makes as elegant a presence as the real Liberace ever did.

TipToe Through The Tulips !!!

Who Ordered This Pizza ! !

JONNY AND CHER & PIZZA.

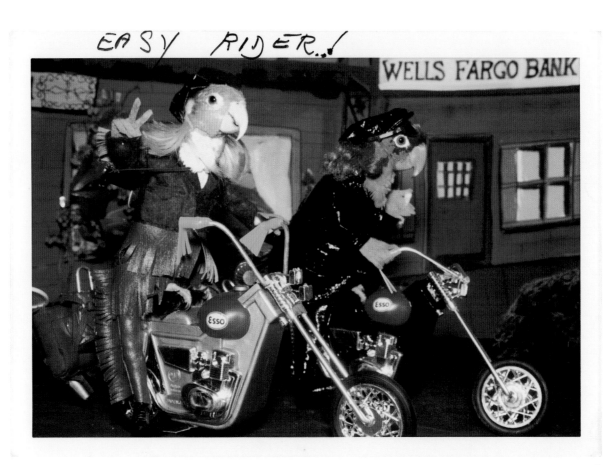

EASY RIDER..!

WELLS FARGO BANK

The Birds From Alcatraz!!

WILD HICKORY NUTS ARE FOR THE BIRDS

SOFT AND DRY !

Madame Butterfly H: H:

10

The Rickshaw !!!

Sherlook Holmes After The Theif

Sherlock Holmes

Freddy The Freeloader

FREDDY the FREELOADER

The Great Battle !!!

General Patton.. 3.

21

HERE COME THE BRIDE...!

22

Honey Mooners

23

"The Couragous Rooster!!"

THE RRODUCER

28

The Greatest Hairdresser

Gcn.Napolean Meets the King

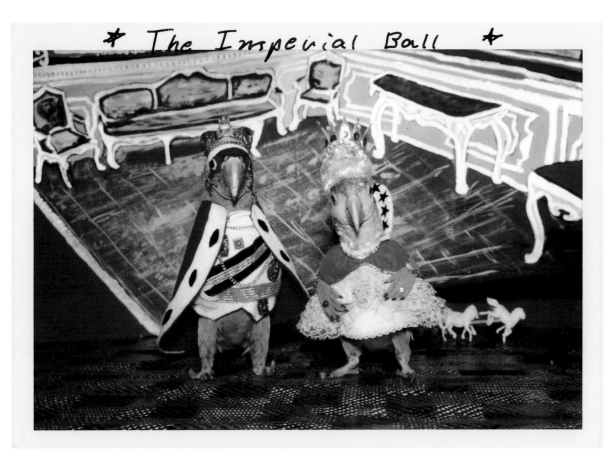

Peter Pan Meets Captain Hook!

Little Red Riding Hood

33

36

BASEBALL.

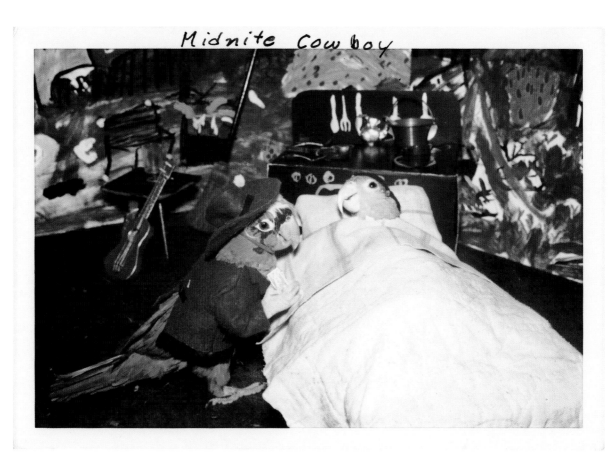

Midnite Cowboy

38

A Boy named "Sue"

Batman and Robin

40

BOATING.

Gen. Custer Meets White Bull! ...

BILLIE JEAN KING + BOBBY RIGGS

Tennis Anyone ?

THE WORLD CHAMPIONS

51

The Championships At Stake!

knockout !!!

THE THREE CABALERRO'S.

THE PUPPET SHOW.

List of Plates

All photographs by Marvin Ballard except where noted. All photograph titles were written by Alba Ballard and are listed as they appear on the original images, including spelling errors and typographic idiosyncracies.

1. Untitled (secretary). Costume and small props by Alba, chair by Marvin, photograph by Paul Anzalone.

2. *Tip-Toe Through the Tulips!!!* Tiny Tim, the ukulele-playing pop singer best known for the 1968 song "Tiptoe Through the Tulips," and his wife, Miss Vicky.

3. *Who Ordered This Pizza!!* Scene from a short film created by Alba and Marvin.

4. *SONNY AND CHER & PIZZA.*

5. *EASY RIDER. . .!* Scene from *Easy Rider,* the 1969 movie starring Peter Fonda and Dennis Hopper.

6. *The Birds From Alcatraz!!* Scene from the 1962 movie *Birdman of Alcatraz,* starring Burt Lancaster.

7. *WILD HICKORY NUTS ARE FOR THE BIRDS.* Inspired by natural food guru Euell Gibbons's commercials for Grape-Nuts cereal.

8. *SOFT AND DRY!* Alba's parody of a 1970s TV commercial for the "woman's deodorant" Soft and Dry.

9. Untitled (Liberace). Costume by Alba, piano by Marvin.

10. *Madame Butterfly.* Scene from Giacomo Puccini's opera.

11. *The Rickshaw!!!* Scene from *Madame Butterfly.*

12. *Sherlock Holmes After the Theif.*

13. *Sherlock Holmes.*

14–15. *Freddy The Freeloader* and *FREDDY the FREELOADER.* Based on the comedian Red Skelton's tramp clown character.

16–20. *General Patton.* Five-image sequence, including *The Great Battle!!!,* based on the 1970 movie *Patton.*

21. *??The Priest's Wife and* [illegible] *??*

22. *HERE COME THE BRIDE..!*

23. *Honey Mooners.*

24. *Nurse Maids.*

25. Untitled (parrot on motorcycle). Costume and small props by Alba, motorcycle by Marvin.

26. *"The Couragous Rooster!!"*

27. *THE DEVIL'S. JUDGEMENT...!*

28. *THE PRODUCER.*

29. *The Greatest Hairdresser.*

30. *Gen. Napolean Meets the King.*

31. ** The Imperial Ball *.*

32. *Peter Pan Meets Captain Hook!*

33. *Little Red Riding Hood.*

34. Untitled (Santa and Mrs. Claus).

35. Untitled (Santa Claus).

36. Untitled (two sailors and a one-legged woman).

37. *Baseball.* The Mets.

38. *Midnite Cowboy.* Reenactment of sickbed scene in 1969 film *Midnight Cowboy,* starring Dustin Hoffman and Jon Voight.

39. *A Boy named "Sue."* Inspired by song written by Shel Silverstein, recorded by Johnny Cash in 1969.

40. *Batman and Robin.*

41. Untitled (Batman, Robin, and The Penguin).

42–43. *BONNIE & CLYDE.* and *BONNIE AND CLYDE.*

44. Untitled (Quasimodo and Esmeralda from *The Hunchback of Notre-Dame*), photograph by Susan Chamberlain.

45. *Mad Scientist.* Photograph from Alba and Marvin's short film *Dr. Frankenstein.*

46. *BOATING.* Photograph from Alba and Marvin's short film based on the movie *Deliverance.*

47. Untitled (parrot standing in front of toy train set tunnel).

48. *Gen. Custer Meets White Bull! . . .*

49. *BILLIE JEAN KING + BOBBY RIGGS.* Reenactment of famous 1973 "Battle of the Sexes" tennis match.

50. *Tennis Anyone?*

51–53. *THE WORLD CHAMPIONS.* Three-image sequence of boxers, including *The Championship's At Stake!* and *Knockout!!!*

54. *THE THREE CABALERRO'S.* Based on the 1944 live-action and animated Disney film *The Three Caballeros,* starring Donald Duck.

55. *THE PUPPET SHOW.*

56–57. Untitled (Jiminy Cricket and Mickey Mouse from *THE PUPPET SHOW).*

58. *BOB HOPE, GOLF, BING CROSBY.*

59. *DEAN MARTIN.* Martin is surrounded by the female ensemble "The Golddiggers," from his television variety show, *The Dean Martin Show.*

Acknowledgments

Special thanks to Deborah Aaronson, Dana Albarella, Paul and Susan Anzalone, Claudio Ballard, Marvin Ballard, Barbara Berkowitz, Susan Chamberlain, Dr. Jonathan Greenfield, Bill Jourdan, Laura Lindgren, The Long Island Parrot Society, Marc Marrone, Christopher Schelling, Jane Searle, Ken Swezey, Elizabeth Taylor, Hap Tivey, Liza Todd Tivey, Lisa Umstead, and Ron Warren.

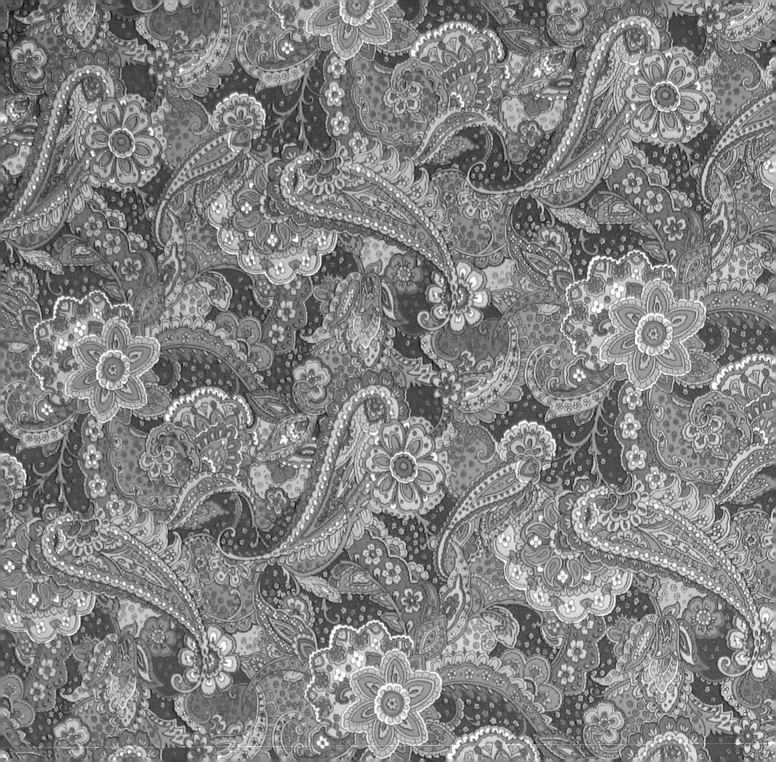